ZONDERVAN | groupware™

If God

G O D

is always

with us,

I S C

why

L O S E

is

R T H A N

he

Y O U T H I

so

N K · J O H N

hard to find?

O R T B E R G

WITH STEPHEN AND AMANDA SORENSON

PARTICIPANT'S GUIDE

ZONDERVAN™

GRAND RAPIDS, MICHIGAN 49530 USA

WILLOW
Willow Creek Resources

ZONDERVAN™

God Is Closer Than You Think Participant's Guide
Copyright © 2005 by John Ortberg

Requests for information should be addressed to:

Zondervan, *Grand Rapids, Michigan 49530*

ISBN-10: 0-310-26639-4
ISBN-13: 978-0-310-26639-6

Interior design by Michelle Espinoza

Printed in the United States of America

05 06 07 08 09 10 11 /❖ DCI/ 10 9 8 7 6 5 4 3 2 1

CONTENTS

SESSION 1:
God's Great Desire for People / 7

SESSION 2:
Where Is God in My World? / 21

SESSION 3:
Partnering with God Today / 35

SESSION 4:
Listening to the Voice of God / 51

SESSION 5:
God Wants a Relationship with You / 67

SESSION 6:
Heaven Breaking Through / 81

God's Great Desire for People

The story of the Bible isn't primarily about the desire of people to be with God: it's the desire of God to be with people.

John Ortberg

Questions to Think About

1. It is one thing for us to talk about how much we want to experience God, but how much do you think God wants to be with us? In what ways do you know God desires a close relationship with you?

2. The Bible says that God reveals himself to us. In what ways can we see, hear, feel, or otherwise recognize God's presence? When does God seem most real to you? What seemingly ordinary things in life have made you aware of his presence?

3. Is it possible for God to be with us here on earth, every day, at every moment—and for us not to be aware of it? Explain your answer.

Video Observations

How close is God?

God looks at us through the eyes of a father

Jacob's story—God shows up where you least expect him

The message of the "bear" story: God is always with us

May the Lord's face shine upon you

Video Discussion

1. How did you relate to the scene of John Ortberg speaking from the top of the tower as being a visual image of the way many of us view God? What other visual images or word pictures would you use to describe the ways in which we view God?

2. When we think of God as being far away, how does that view impact our relationship with him?

3. What did you think or feel when John Ortberg talked about God looking at each of us with the loving eyes of a father, like the father with his son's photograph on his screensaver?

4. What if God is really all around us—and we don't realize it? What might we be missing if God, like the adult bear snarling at the mountain lion, really is closer than we think?

5. Michelangelo's fresco of Adam and God in the Sistine Chapel represents the perspective that the Bible is about God's desire to be with people rather than our desire to be with God. In what ways does this perspective change your perception of your relationship with God? What practical difference might this new perspective make in your life?

Group Exploration

1. The story of the Bible is the story of God's desire to be with people. He extends himself, reaching out to us today just as he has since the day he created Adam. Let's explore together God's desire to be with us and the impact it can have on our lives.

   a. What does the psalmist David say about God's knowledge of us and his actions toward us? (See Psalm 139:1–10.) What does this reveal about God's desire for relationship with us?

   b. Psalm 89 gives us a picture of the kind of relationship God can have with his people and his people can have with him. Read verses 15–17 and 19–28 and note some of the qualities of a close relationship with God. Part of this psalm refers specifically to David, who had a remarkable relationship with God, but use the images in this psalm to discuss what a close relationship with God might look like in our lives today.

2. In the video, John Ortberg shared stories that illustrate the heart, character, and commitment of a loving father—the father who kept his son's photograph on his screensaver, the story about the bear cub. In what ways do the following Scripture passages show us that God is our ever-present, loving Father?

Scripture Passage	God as Our Father
Psalm 145:17–19	
Psalm 46:1–3	
Psalm 32:8; Isaiah 42:16	
Psalm 103:8–14	
James 1:17	

3. God's most frequent promise in Scripture is "I will be with you."
   Let's consider several situations in which God gave that promise
   and discuss how God's promise to be with us applies to us in similar situations.

   a. Note the survival challenge Isaac faced, what God told him to
      do, and what God promised (Genesis 26:1–6). What kinds of
      external circumstances can cause us to be afraid? What
      changes when we realize that God is with us in these situations?

   b. Twice in Joshua 1:1–9 God tells Joshua he will be with him!
      What monumental task did Joshua face? What were God's
      instructions and promises related to that task? What impact
      can God's presence have on our feelings of insecurity when
      he gives us a seemingly overwhelming assignment?

   c. What threatening situation did the apostle Paul face in Acts
      18:5–11? What did God tell Paul to do, and what did God
      promise? When we face painful challenges or uncertainty,
      what reassurance do we need from God to press on? How
      might we view sharing our faith differently if we know God
      stands with us?

4. No matter how often we read that God will be with us, there are times when we may not be able to see him, times when we are convinced that he is nowhere to be found.

    a. Read 2 Kings 6:8–18 to see how the prophet Elisha's servant found out that God is indeed closer than we think! Talk about how this experience can help open our eyes to God's presence in our lives—even in the most unlikely circumstances.

    b. If you have time, consider two other instances in Scripture when God was far closer than his people realized: Gideon in the winepress (Judges 6:1–16) and the two disciples on the Emmaus Road (Luke 24:13–35). Talk about how God might "show up" in your life in unexpected ways.

5. Jesus came to earth as "Immanuel," which means "God with us." His life gives us an incomparable example of a life lived in the presence of God. The following verses reveal how the presence of God impacted the daily life of Jesus—his thoughts, actions, and attitudes. Read each passage and discuss how our daily lives would be different if we also sought to live in the presence of God.

    a. Everything Jesus did was a result of God's power. (See John 13:3.)

b.   Jesus was committed to doing God's work on earth. (See John 5:17.)

c.   Jesus said what the Father told him to say. (See John 12:49–50.)

6.   Read Matthew 28:18–20, often called the Great Commission. What were Jesus' instructions and his promise to his disciples? What difference did that promise make in their lives? What difference should it make in our lives today?

Personal Journey: To Do Now

1. The story of the Bible is the story of God's desire to be with people. He is determined that each of us be his friend, his companion, and his dwelling place. He is stretching out to reach us and fill our lives with his presence. All it takes is the barest effort—the lifting of a finger, the whisper of a prayer—for us to reach him.

    a. Michelangelo's portrayal of God and Adam on the ceiling of the Sistine Chapel illustrates God's determination to reach out so that every human being can experience life in his presence. He longs for us to respond to him and close the tiny gap that remains between us. When in your life have you become aware of the gap between yourself and God? What was your response to God, and what was the result? What may be keeping you from "lifting a finger" in response to God?

    b. Think about times in life when you have felt God's presence with you, then consider times when his presence seemed elusive. How did your thoughts and feelings toward God differ during those contrasting circumstances? In what ways might you have thought or felt differently if you had a clearer picture of God's desire to reach out to you (as in Michelangelo's portrayal of God reaching out to Adam)?

2. God is closer than we think—amazingly close. The most frequent promise in the Bible is, "I will be with you." That promise, that God is always present, always watching, and always protecting makes all the difference. It gives us the courage to face life in a rocky, stormy world.

    a. Life hinges on the promise of God's presence with us—courage, guidance, and hope all reside with him. As you interacted with Scripture and other group members during the Group Exploration time, which particular aspect(s) of God's presence made the greatest impact on you? Why?

    b. How might your life be different—your view of yourself, your thoughts, your relationships, your actions, your hopes, your fears—if you truly believe that God is closer than you think, if you live life knowing that God has you on his screensaver and is watching your every move with pride and joy?

3. Spiritual growth is the process of learning to increase our capacity to experience God's presence. It is learning to partner together with God during the ordinary moments of our ordinary lives. There are guiding principles that will help us practice God's presence in our daily lives.

    a. We long for the reality that Moses prayed for: "The LORD bless you and keep you; the LORD make his face shine upon you" (Numbers 6:24–25). How might your life be different if you actually lived in the reality that God's face is turned toward you?

    b. What are your expectations concerning this study? What would you like to experience, learn, or feel in relationship to God's presence in your life? Prayerfully consider what may be limiting your ability to see him and ask him to open your eyes to his presence in your everyday life.

Personal Journey: To Do on Your Own

It is possible for each of us to learn how to recognize and experience God's presence—right now, every moment, wherever we are. There's no better time than right now to begin living with an awareness of God's presence in your life. Set aside time during the next few days to read each of the following guiding principles for practicing God's presence every day. Between now and the next session, think about them, pray about them, and ask God to open your heart and mind to his presence.

- God is *always* present and active in my life, whether or not I see him.
- Coming to recognize and experience God's presence is *learned* behavior; I can cultivate it.
- My task is to meet God in *this* moment.
- I am always tempted to live "outside" this moment. When I do that, I lose my sense of God's presence.
- Sometimes God seems far away for reasons I do not understand. Those moments, too, are opportunities to learn.
- Whenever I fail, I can always start again right away.
- No one knows the full extent to which a human being can experience God's presence.
- My desire for God ebbs and flows, but his desire for me is constant.
- Every thought carries a "spiritual charge" that moves me a little closer to or a little farther from God.
- Every aspect of my life—work, relationships, hobbies, errands— is of immense and genuine interest to God.
- My path to experiencing God's presence will not look quite like anyone else's.
- Straining and trying too hard do not help.

Where Is God in My World?

God wants to be known, but not in a way that overwhelms us, that takes away the possibility of love freely chosen. . . . He often shows up in unexpected ways. He travels incognito. . . . You never know where he'll turn up, or whom he'll speak through, or what unlikely scenario he'll use for his purpose.

John Ortberg

Questions to Think About

1. Postcards from California may advertise endless sunshine, but the truth is, there are cloudy, gray days—even in sunny California. What do we tend to expect the "postcards" of daily life with God to look like? Do we expect sun-drenched beaches or drizzle-choked freeways? How do those expectations affect the real experience of our daily walk with him? Why might we sense God's presence more clearly at one time in life than another?

2. When two people are in similar situations, God's presence may be clearly visible to one person, but mysteriously elusive to the other. What do you think could account for the difference in their experience?

3. What if every day were bright and sunny, filled with unbelievable goodness and meaning, and we saw God clearly at every turn? In what ways would that be a good thing? In what ways might that not be such a good thing? If you feel comfortable doing so, describe a time when you felt particularly close to God. What made that time meaningful or life-changing?

Video Observations

"Rainbow" days

"Ordinary" days

"Don't look at me, God" days

"Mystery" days

Sitting at the feet of Jesus

Video Discussion

1. As John Ortberg spoke about the four kinds of days—rainbow days; ordinary days; "Don't look at me, God" days; and mystery days—what insights did you gain into the kinds of days you have experienced?

2. In what ways do you think a person's passion to know God and experience his presence changes as the newness of his or her relationship with Jesus wears off?

3. John Ortberg spoke of the risks of "spiritual habituation" when we experience ordinary days. Identify and discuss some of those risks. What kinds of things can help us cultivate an awareness of God during such times? How can such times encourage our spiritual growth?

4. How do we tend to respond to God when we are truly seeking his presence, but he seems elusive? In what ways do you agree or disagree with John Ortberg's assessment that there is a "good of not knowing"? What do you see as the value of not knowing?

5. What might it mean, in practical terms in our day, to "sit at the feet of Jesus"? What kinds of things keep us from sitting at Jesus' feet and being "covered by the dust of our rabbi"?

Group Exploration

1. People in the Bible experienced rainbow days when God made his presence known and they felt great! Consider the following rainbow days:

    a. Rainbow days are the result of a promise God made to his faithful servant, Noah. Read about the first rainbow day in Genesis 6:9–13, 17–19; 9:8–16. God intends the rainbow to remind us of what important relationship?

    b. The day King Solomon dedicated the temple was an incredible rainbow day! Note Solomon's prayer, God's response, and the result. (See 2 Chronicles 6:40–42; 7:1–4, 8–10.) What do we learn about rainbow days from this passage?

    c. Discuss the role of rainbow days in our lives today. What are our expectations of rainbow days? In what ways might our expectations differ from God's intent as described in the previous two Scripture passages?

2. The Bible also records plenty of ordinary days and mystery days
    when it was much more difficult—perhaps nearly impossible—for
    people to feel God's presence. Yet over and over again, we see that
    God was present indeed.

    a. Read 1 Kings 19:1–8. What kind of day was Elijah having?
        How did God show Elijah how close he was when Elijah fled
        from Jezebel?

    b. What were David's thoughts about God's presence with him
        in Psalm 13? What was David doing about it? In what way(s)
        do you think this action might have affected his awareness of
        God's presence? How do you think your awareness of God's
        presence would change if you responded the same way?

    c. What kind of day did David describe in Psalm 69:1–3? How
        close do you think David considered God to be in those cir-
        cumstances? (See Psalm 69:13–18.)

d. What kind of a problem did Habakkuk have in perceiving God's presence? (See Habakkuk 1:2–4.) How do we know God was right there in the midst of things? (See Habakkuk 1:5.)

3. John Ortberg wrote that after we have been Christians for a while, "God takes away the props so that we can begin to grow true devotion that is strong enough to carry on even when unaided by emotions." With this thought in mind, discuss what purpose God could have intended for each of the ordinary or mystery days mentioned in Question 2.

4. As a group, identify some things we can do to learn to see God in the ordinary, rather than being dependent on the extraordinary. Then, read the following Scripture passages and write down the ways God encourages us to seek his presence.

Scripture Passage	Ways to Seek God's Presence
1 Chronicles 16:10–12	
Psalm 20:6–7	
1 Thessalonians 5:17	
Hebrews 10:22–23	

5. How does the God who is closer than we think promise to respond when we seek him? (See Psalm 9:10; Isaiah 42:16; Luke 11:10.)

6. When we can't see God clearly, our initial response often is to ask, "Where is God? Why is he hiding from me? Why has he left me?" But sometimes the question we need to be asking is a more difficult one: "What have I done to separate myself from God's presence?"

    a. What did Adam and Eve do when they realized God was near? Why? (See Genesis 3:8–13.)

    b. What was Jonah's first response to God's message? (See Jonah 1:1–3.)

    c. What do we think we are accomplishing when we, like Adam and Eve and Jonah, say, in effect, "Don't look at me, God"? What impact does pushing God away have on our spiritual growth? Discuss why it is sometimes more appealing to push God away rather than face our sin and have him near us.

7. What impact does sin have on God's presence with us? (See Psalm 5:4; Isaiah 59:1–2; 1 Peter 3:12.)

Personal Journey: To Do Now

1. Sometimes we have rainbow days when God's presence breaks through and overwhelms us with joy, glory, meaning, and goodness. We love those days. They are precious gifts to store up for the days when God isn't as easy to see.

    a. Write very briefly about several rainbow days God has given you. In what ways did those days cause your relationship with God to flourish? How would reflecting on God's presence during those days help you face days when no rainbow is in sight?

    b. Think about the days when you have really sensed God's presence. What was taking place in your life and in your relationship with God that seemed to make you more aware of his presence?

2. Sometimes it is more difficult to experience the presence of God. On ordinary days, God is still there, but his presence isn't center stage. On other days, God is even more elusive and we may not even know why. During these times, we need to learn to walk by faith, not by sight.

a. When have you wished that God would show himself more plainly? How has God used those times of uncertainty to build your trust in him? to push you to learn more of what it means to walk by faith and not by sight?

b. In *God Is Closer Than You Think,* John Ortberg mentioned several warning signs of running on "spiritual autopilot" rather than being refreshed daily by God's presence. These included worrying about money or your job, yelling at the kids, and being jealous or judgmental. What are your top warning signs of spiritual habituation or running on autopilot?

3. Days that are not rainbow days may be God's doing. Perhaps he wants us to learn to pay closer attention to him, to trust his presence even when we don't see it, or to find rainbow moments in ordinary days. Sometimes the absence of rainbow days is our doing. We may be distracted from seeking God's presence, or we may be hiding from God's presence and pushing him away because of sin.

a. Sometimes no matter how hard we try, we can't seem to find God's presence the way we hope to find it. Think of such times in your life and consider why God allowed you to face such uncertainty. What might God be trying to teach you during those times when he seems hidden?

b. John Ortberg talked about times when we want to *hide* from God, when we don't want him around. When do you find yourself not wanting God around? Which thoughts or activities tempt you to pray, "Don't look at me, God"? In what ways do sin and distractions diminish your capacity to experience God?

Personal Journey: To Do on Your Own

Jesus gently but relentlessly asked people to make a decision about their relationship with him. It is no different for us. In order to live in Jesus' presence, to sit at his feet, we must ask him to be our teacher and companion in every moment of life.

How do we do this? One way is to "review the dailies." This simply means we take the time and effort to review the previous day and see where God was present—how he appeared and how he worked in each moment. We look and listen to how God was speaking to us through those scenes. We review what we thought about and how we responded. We consider what we could do to improve. By reviewing the "dailies," we increase our capacity to pay attention to God and his presence.

So why not give this a try? You can begin to "review the dailies" with God by answering the following questions about yesterday:

- What were my first thoughts?
- How did I respond to people around me? to God? (Note patterns of response.)
- How much time did I spend seeking God's presence?
- Where was God present and at work in each scene of my day—family, breakfast, work, interactions with neighbors and children, and so on.
- How might God have been speaking to me through those scenes?
- What can I learn from yesterday that might help me become more aware of God's presence today?
- What happened for which I can be thankful (a rainbow moment)?
- Which pattern(s) should I evaluate—and possibly work to improve?
- Did I have any moments when I really wanted to hide from God, when I didn't want him around?

Partnering with God Today

The greatest moment of your life is now. Not because it's pleasant or happy or easy, but because this moment is . . . where God is. If you are going to be with God at all, you must be with him now—*in this moment.*

John Ortberg

Questions to Think About

1. How highly do you tend to value the present moment? Do you value it more or less than the past or future? How would you respond if someone said to you, "*This*—right now—is the greatest moment of your life"? Why?

2. Sometimes we put off living with a sense of God's presence today and say we'll start doing it *tomorrow.* In what ways does it matter whether we begin living in God's presence today or tomorrow?

3. We have all heard and recited the phrase from the Lord's prayer, "Thy will be done." What have you thought that phrase means? What does that phrase have to do with you and your life?

Video Observations

Another day with the frogs

This is the day to experience God's presence

The message of "as you wish"

Aligning ourselves with God's Spirit

Spending ordinary days with God

Video Discussion

1. When Moses asked Pharaoh when he wanted the frogs to be gone, he replied, "Tomorrow." What surprises you about Pharaoh's response? Why do you think he was willing to put up with the frogs for another day?

2. In what ways do we behave like Pharaoh and put up with a less-than-satisfying spiritual life when we could experience a rich, full life with God? Why do we procrastinate spiritually?

3. What kinds of expectations do we think need to be met, or what things do we feel must be in place before we can begin our great adventure of partnering with God? What is the fallacy of thinking that someday life will be different?

4. What is it about a heart attitude that says, "As you wish" to God that is so powerful? What difference can the words "as you wish" make in our everyday, ordinary lives?

5. John Ortberg described a "disconnect" that many of us feel between life experienced in partnership with God and the ordinary moments of daily life. Discuss the ways you feel this disconnect. How might those experiences be different if you learned to live them with God?

Group Exploration

1. Scripture gives us ample instruction on how important it is to live life with God as well as specific instruction on how to do it. Which fundamental principles for living life with God are emphasized in Ephesians 5:15–17?

2. Sometimes we are aware of the choice before us—to align ourselves with God or to pursue our own way—but we don't want to commit to a choice; we'd rather procrastinate. Yet procrastination is a risky option.

   a. What does God warn us about regarding tomorrow, and what is his terminology for procrastination on spiritual decisions? (See Proverbs 27:1; James 4:13–17.) In God's eyes, does *today* make a difference? What is your response to God's assessment of procrastination as described in these passages?

   b. The Bible provides many examples of people who had to choose whether or not they would align themselves with God. Read the following passages, noting the opportunities God made available and what can be lost when people do not respond to him *today.*

Scripture Passage	Opportunities Lost by Procrastination
Matthew 4:18–22; 8:19–23	
Genesis 19:15–17, 23–26	
Matthew 25:1–10	
Luke 19:41–44	

   c.   What kinds of opportunities do we miss out on today because
        of spiritual procrastination?

3. How do we know that God knows us, is willing to be with us, and is involved in the details of our lives? (See Matthew 6:7–8; John 1:47–48; Acts 17:24–28.)

4. Jesus is our example of how to live all of life in the presence of God. The attitude of his heart before God was always, "As you wish."

    a. What was Jesus' purpose in coming to earth? (See Hebrews 10:5–9.)

    b. What sustained Jesus as he went about his life on earth? (See John 4:31–34; 6:35–40.)

    c. What did Jesus do to align his heart with the heart of God before he called his disciples? (See Luke 6:12–13.)

d. How far was Jesus willing to go in his commitment to do God's will? (See Mark 14:32–36.)

e. Discuss ways in which the example of Jesus teaches, inspires, or encourages you to partner with God in your daily life.

5. When we choose to say "Thy will be done" rather than "My will be done" we open our hearts to the presence of God. What do we receive from God when we choose to align ourselves with him? (See Ephesians 3:16–19; 1 John 2:15–17.)

6. A key aspect of remaining in God's presence is knowing what to do when we sin, when we forget or refuse to be conduits of God's Spirit. John Ortberg used a surfing image to help us see how God always sends us another wave, another opportunity to confess our sin and reconnect with him. In what ways do the following Scripture passages show that God is ready to forgive so we can get up and try again? (See Lamentations 3:22–23; Psalm 32:5; Proverbs 28:13; Micah 7:18.)

Personal Journey: To Do Now

1. This moment is the greatest moment of your life because it is the only moment—not the past, not the future—you actually have to be with God. God offers to be with you in whatever you face, but this is his day. Now is the time to align yourself with God's Spirit and surrender to his wishes.

    a. Read Psalm 118:24, then write down what is valuable and important about *this* day. Ask God to help you value *this* moment. Ask him to be present in everything you do the rest of today.

    b. What specific things might God want to do in and through you *this* day? (At work? at home? with a family member? with a friend?)

2. The most dangerous word is tomorrow. We may recognize the danger of saying "no" to God, but we may not be as aware of the danger of saying "tomorrow." Yet procrastination not only leads us to tolerate and maintain destructive behavioral patterns, it keeps us from being fully present with God. If we are ever going to experience God's presence, it has to be now, not tomorrow.

a. It's time for a "frog hunt." Identify any "frogs" you are living with right now—work addiction? bitterness? broken relationships? fear? anger? In what way(s) have you chosen to "live with the frogs" rather than being more fully present with God?

b. When have you put off getting serious about your life with God, and why? What excuses have you made? (Be honest!) What would your life look like if you had chosen to act rather than procrastinate? What are you willing to do about it *today*?

3. Every moment of every day we each make a crucial choice: our hearts assume a "Thy will be done" or "My will be done" posture. The heart that learns to say, "Thy will be done, I will do as you wish," from one moment to the next is the heart that opens itself to the presence of God.

   a. What is the predominant attitude of your heart? Is it "as you wish," or is it "my will be done"?

b. What do you truly want your heart attitude to be moment by
    moment throughout each day? Write down several things—
    thoughts, deeds, character issues—that may be keeping you
    from having that attitude. Which practical step(s) are you will-
    ing to take today to more closely align your heart attitude with
    God and allow his Spirit to flow through you?

Personal Journey: To Do on Your Own

Spending the day with God does not necessarily involve doing different activities than you already do. It involves learning to do what you already do in a different way—doing it with God. It means acknowledging your dependence on God, telling him about your concerns, and inviting him to share each moment of the day with you.

1. Think about your typical, ordinary day and consider how you can invite God to participate with you during each and every moment. Use the chart on the following pages as a guide to focus your thoughts and actions, then try an "I'm going to live this day with God" experiment. Acknowledge your dependence on God and invite him to spend the day with you.

2. Sometimes when we fail to keep open the flow of the Holy Spirit in our lives, we are tempted to beat ourselves up for it. But John Ortberg emphasized how important it is to recognize God's mercy and get ready to "do it right" the next time. What kinds of things keep you from reconnecting with God quickly after you sin? In which area(s) of your life do you need to admit your failure, confess your sin, and through the forgiveness and power of God get right back up and keep going?

My Daily Tasks	How I Can Do These Tasks with God
Waking up	
Washing up	
Working	
Eating	
Taking a break	
Waiting in line	

Driving	
Solving a problem	
Dealing with an interruption	
Working out at the gym	
Doing homework with my kids	
Cleaning up after dinner	
Reading/watching TV	

Listening to the Voice of God

Every thought is either enabling and strengthening you to . . . live a kingdom kind of life, or robbing you of that life. Every thought is— at least to a small extent—God-breathed or God-avoidant; leading to death or leading toward life.

John Ortberg

Questions to Think About

1. What kinds of thoughts and images enter our minds on a daily basis? In what ways do some of those thoughts and images tend to distort our view of life and scramble our perception of God?

2. What role does the mind play in our relationship with God? In what ways does God speak to us through our minds, and how can we each cultivate a mind that is in tune with God?

3. What happens to our minds when we hold on to thoughts related to our problems, failures, anger, fear, bitterness, and the like? How much control can we exert over such thoughts? How, for example, can we decide whether or not to pay attention to fear or anger, or whether to allow resentful or bitter thoughts to dominate our minds?

Video Observations

We all hear voices

Recognizing the voice of God

What kind of mind do we want to have?

Cultivating a mind where God dwells

If you can worry, you can meditate

Video Discussion

1. To what extent are our minds a bit like Dugan the dog—running toward every voice that calls to us? What happens to us spiritually when we, like Dugan, listen to too many voices and run in a dozen directions at once?

2. What are some of the "voices"—good as well as bad—that clamor for our attention? What are some guidelines that can help us determine whether the voice we hear is the voice of God?

3. John Ortberg says that if we can worry, we can meditate! In what ways is this true? What is the key difference between worry and meditation? Why is meditation on Scripture a key part of learning to listen to God's voice?

4. John Ortberg pointed out the "dance" that bowlers do after they let go of the ball. How does the bowling image help you remember to "let go" of your problems, concerns, and failures and put them in God's hands so that he can dwell in your mind?

5. What role can other people in the Christian community play to help us cultivate a mind that dwells on God? In what ways have you experienced this level of sharing and support? What keeps us from doing this more?

Group Exploration

1. God wants each of us to have a beautiful mind—a mind attuned to his voice and filled with his life-giving thoughts! But there is an ongoing battle for control of our minds. Note what the following Scripture passages tell us about the battlefield of the mind.

   a. What are the two entities vying for control of the mind, and where does each lead? (See Romans 8:5–6.)

   b. What terminology does the apostle Paul use to describe the conflict for control of the mind? (See Romans 7:21–23.) Why is this significant?

2. Scripture is very clear about the kind of mind we naturally develop if we do not cultivate a mind that listens to God. Read the following passages and note what a mind without God is like.

Scripture Passage	The Natural Mind without God
Psalm 10:4	
Ephesians 4:17–18	
Romans 8:7–8	
Philippians 3:18–19	

3. If we want to follow our natural tendency, or as John Ortberg says, "If our goal is debauchery, lechery, and depravity," we don't have to do much. But what does Scripture warn us about if our goal is to have a mind that is the dwelling place of God? (See 2 Corinthians 11:3.)

4. Sometimes we think we can dabble in what Scripture calls "double-mindedness," choosing positive spiritual input when we feel like it, but focusing on whatever else is out there at other times.

   a. When it comes to hearing God's voice and living in his presence, what is the truth about double-mindedness? (See Luke 16:13; James 1:5–8.)

   b. Discuss the results John Ortberg mentioned of being double-minded. Why would a person choose this option? What does James 4:7–8 tell us is the cure for being double-minded?

5. Since our natural tendency is to avoid God's presence and shut out his voice, we obviously have some work to do if we are to cultivate a mind that is receptive to him.

   a. What do we need before we can have a mind that is the dwelling place of God? (See 1 Corinthians 2:11–16.)

b. What needs to happen to our mind so that it can be the dwelling place of God? (See Romans 12:2.)

c. How do we fill our mind with the good things God says are important to keeping attuned to his voice? (See Matthew 22:37; Philippians 4:8–9; Colossians 3:16; Hebrews 3:1.)

d. What is the result of a heart that listens to God's voice and a mind that is receptive to God's presence? (See Philippians 4:4–7.)

Personal Journey: To Do Now

1. All of us hear voices that influence our thoughts and shape our lives. Some voices are true, some are false. Some thoughts lead to life, some lead to death. God's desire is for us to listen to his voice so that our minds will be permeated by his life-giving thoughts.

    a. No thought is purely neutral. Every thought is God-breathed or God-avoidant, either moving us in the direction of life or shutting us off to the presence of God and leading toward death. Make a list of the kind of thoughts you tend to entertain—God-avoidant as well as God-breathed.

My God-Breathed Thoughts	My God-Avoidant Thoughts

b.   Which thoughts are more predominant or exert a stronger influence in your life?

2.   The voices we listen to and the thoughts we allow to occupy our minds eventually shape who we become and what we do. If our goal is debauchery, lechery, and depravity, we don't have to do much—just avoid God, avoid Scripture, and avoid godly people. If our goal is a mediocre spiritual life, we can go for the double-minded deal—occasionally focus on positive spiritual input and the rest of the time focus on whatever else is out there. If our goal is to have a mind that is the dwelling place of God, we need to fill it with what God says.

a.   Take another look at your God-breathed and God-avoidant thoughts from the previous chart and write down the impact those thoughts are having on your life. Consider how much you desire to have a mind that is permeated with God's life-giving thoughts.

b.   Think about the main sources of your thoughts. In what ways is your mind being filled with positive spiritual input? How much is it being filled with other things? What changes do you need to make to cultivate your mind on the things of God?

3. Those who practice God's presence have learned to listen to God's voice. They have learned to say "yes" when God speaks, which increases their sensitivity to hearing him the next time. They have cultivated a mind that is receptive to God's presence.

   a. Why is it so important for you to recognize God's voice among the many "voices" that clamor for your attention every day?

   b. How much effort do you put into hearing and responding to God's voice? How you might improve in this area? Be specific!

Personal Journey: To Do on Your Own

Only God can transform a mind and give it new thoughts, but God-centered meditation is a process that helps us have a mind that stores up good things. Meditation involves dwelling with some intensity and duration on a particular thought or image. Meditation helps us realize that God is with us and that we're tuned in to him.

1. Think about areas of your life in which you are still holding on to problems, challenges, failures, or pain instead of letting go and asking God to transform your mind with his thoughts. Use the chart on the following page as a starting point.

2. Meditation on Scripture is perhaps the oldest and most powerful practice for learning to listen for God's voice. Make Psalm 16:8 the focus of your meditation this week: "I have set the LORD always before me. Because he is at my right hand, I will not be shaken." As you go through each day, focus on the thought that God is with you in all that you do. As you face problems, remind yourself that you have put God in first place. When all is going well, remember that God is a part of it. The chart on page 65 is a helpful reminder of the truths discussed in this session.

My Life	Problems, Challenges, Failures I Need to Let Go	How God's Thoughts Can Help Cultivate a Beautiful Mind
Family and friends		
Work		
Key relationships		
God		
Church		
Finances		
Health		
Hopes and dreams		

Cultivate Your Mind: It's Your Choice!		
Follow Your "Natural" Tendency	**Go for the "Half-and-Half" Deal**	**Cultivate a Mind That Is Receptive to God**
Avoid Scripture	Dabble in Scripture	Meditate on Scripture
Avoid wise, honest, and godly people	Receive sporadic spiritual input	Seek out wise, honest, and godly people
Avoid honest self-examination	Indulge in hidden debauchery	Pursue honest self-examination
Stay away from church or Christian fellowship	Go to church sometimes	Seek out a good church and Christian fellowship
Don't bother to pray	Pray sporadically, particularly when you are in trouble	Pray when things are good as well as when they are bad
Be self-centered	Think about God occasionally	Celebrate God's presence

God Wants a Relationship with You

Every human being you ever see was made in the image of God, and Jesus says that if we want, he will come and make his home in us. So we're never to look at another person without having a sense of awe and reverence that says, "This is one in whom God may dwell."

John Ortberg

Questions to Think About

1. The story of Father Damien serves as a reminder of what Jesus did for us: Jesus came down from heaven, became one of us, and lived among us. How does Jesus' incarnation—his coming to earth to live with us—communicate God's desire to have a relationship with us? What impact does it have on our everyday life?

2. What does it mean to be made in God's image, to actually be a dwelling place for God? What difference does it make in terms of how we view ourselves and what we do? What difference does it make in terms of how we view other people and our relationships with them?

3. To what extent do we see and hear God through the actions and words of ordinary people we encounter in everyday life? If you feel comfortable doing so, talk about one of your experiences.

Video Observations

The Bible's definition of "church"

The many ways we connect with God

    Intellectual

    Relational

    Serving

Worship

Activist

Contemplative

Creation

We are God's dwelling place

Video Discussion

1. How does the Bible use the word *church?* What is the significant difference between how *church* is used in Scripture and how we tend to use it?

2. What kinds of things has Jesus said that indicate he truly is present in his followers? Why is this important to us today? In what ways might the fact that Jesus is present wherever his people gather change the nature of our gatherings and the way we view one another?

3. As John Ortberg talked about various spiritual pathways, what insights did you gain into the ways in which you connect with God? What did you learn about how you become aware of his presence and grow spiritually? What insight did you gain into how other people close to you—family members, people in your church, friends—connect with God?

4. Our response to other people sometimes indicates that we view one spiritual pathway as better than another. Are some pathways better than others? Why or why not?

5. If we recognize that people have the capacity to be carriers of God's presence and that one of the most powerful ways we experience God is through people, how might our interactions with one another change?

Group Exploration

1. God loves us so much that Jesus came to earth to live among us and help us see God. What do each of the following Scripture passages reveal about Jesus and his efforts to connect with us while he lived on earth?

   a. What was Jesus willing to do in order to connect with us? (See Philippians 2:5–8.)

   b. How well does Jesus understand what we go through in life, and what does he offer us? (See Hebrews 4:14–16.)

   c. When Jesus lived among us, what did he show us, and what was the impact on the world around him? (See John 1:10–14.)

2. When Jesus went back to heaven, he said the Holy Spirit would form a new community that would become his new body, his presence in the world.

   a. Read each of the following passages and note what the Bible says about God's presence among Jesus' followers today.

Scripture Passage	God's Presence Today
Romans 8:9–11	
1 Corinthians 3:16–17	
Colossians 1:24–27	

   b. Romans 12:3–8 and 1 Corinthians 12:27–28 also refer to Jesus' followers as being a part of his body, the church, which is his presence on earth. What else do these passages mention that relates to how people experience God's presence? In what ways do these gifts reflect our uniqueness in God's creation? What is the relationship between the kinds of gifts mentioned in these passages and the spiritual pathways John Ortberg describes?

3. We may be inclined to overlook or minimize the powerful ways we experience God's presence through people, but the writers of Scripture say some truly remarkable things about God being present in and through us. Carefully consider the following examples of how other people help us experience the presence of God.

    a. Read Matthew 18:19–20. What is surprising about the promise Jesus makes? What difference does it make in how you approach prayer and fellowship with other believers?

    b. Read Matthew 25:35–40. When we serve others in need, how aware are we of the fact that we are actually serving Jesus? How might we serve differently if we viewed ourselves as serving Jesus?

    c. Read 1 John 4:12. In what ways might our day change as we remember the fact that God actually lives in us when we love others?

4. God often sends his messages through ordinary people who may not impress us as being God-bearers. Let's consider a classic example of a person who had difficulty hearing God's voice from the mouths of ordinary people. (See 2 Kings 5.)

a.   Who was Naaman, and what difficulty did he face (v. 1)?

b.   Who did God first use to convey a message of hope to Naa-man (vv. 2–3)? Was there anything about this person that would have convinced Naaman that she was a God-bearer? Explain your answer.

c.   Next, Naaman received a clear message from God, but how did he respond, and why (vv. 9–12)?

d.   Who did God use to reach out to Naaman one last time, and what happened (vv. 13–14)?

e. How do we know Naaman finally got the message (vv. 15–18)? Talk about how the story might have turned out if even one of these obscure God-bearers had refused to communicate God's message to Naaman. Who are the Naamans in your life, and how has God called you to reveal himself to them?

Personal Journey: To Do Now

1. There is no one-size-fits-all way to draw close to God. God created you, knows you, and wants to have a relationship with you that is unlike his relationship with any other being. He connects with each of us in ways that correspond to the way he wired us.

    a. Which spiritual pathway(s) are most meaningful to you in connecting with God? How are you incorporating practices that involve these pathways into the rhythms of your life?

    b. What can you do to be more appreciative of people whose spiritual pathways are quite different from yours?

2. The miracle of the Incarnation is that God came to earth as one of us in order to connect with us. But an even greater miracle is the fact that after Jesus ascended into heaven, he became present on earth through the people who follow him. So when it comes to people, God really is closer than you think!

    a. When you open your eyes to the truth that other people are God-carriers just as you are, what is your response? How might your actions and attitudes change when you see God's presence in another person?

b. In what ways have other people helped you see God's presence in new ways? In what ways has God used you to reveal his presence to other people?

3. People are the only creatures in the universe made in the image of God. So people are not God's "Plan B" for connecting with us; God intends our relationships with other people to play a role in connecting us with him. We need to recognize our role as God-carriers and look for God's presence and listen for his voice in the people around us.

a. Which person(s) in your life might you be overlooking and thereby missing an opportunity to experience more of God's presence?

b. Think about your daily encounters with other people and ask, "Is my interaction characterized by a 'Do I like you, or do I need you?' response or a 'Can I help you find God?' response?" How might you want those encounters to change?

Personal Journey: To Do on Your Own

How well do you do at looking for God's presence and listening for his messages in the people around you? Perhaps now is the time to consider changes you may need to make in your actions and attitudes in this area. Try the assignment John Ortberg asked you to take on this week: For one day, look and listen for God in each person you see.

- When you see a difficult person, hear Jesus saying, "Love your enemy, pray for those who persecute you."
- When you see a needy person, hear, "Whatever you did for the least of these . . . you did for me."
- When you see someone you love, allow God to love you through that person.
- When someone confronts you, ask God if perhaps he is speaking to you.
- When you see a stranger, remember the "Can I help you?" prayer.
- When you see a fellow believer, hear Jesus saying, "Wherever two or three come together in my name, there I am with them."

Heaven Breaking Through

Many people think that Jesus came to earth to die on the cross, but that was just part of his mission. His overall mission was to bring the reality of God's presence and power to earth and to invite us to join him in making things down here run the way they do up there.

John Ortberg

Questions to Think About

1. When John Ortberg said that "spiritual winter" doesn't get the last word, what do you think he meant? What does get the last word? Why is it important for us to know that there is something beyond this life, beyond seasons of spiritual winter?

2. What is the good news that Jesus came to earth to proclaim? In what practical ways does it make a difference in our ordinary, everyday life?

3. What convinces you that God really exists, that he is good, and that he is with us in this life?

Video Observations

What's on the other side of the hedge?

The man who came from the other side

The kingdom has arrived—right here, right now

Making "up there" come "down here"

God is closer than you think—even during spiritual winter

Video Discussion

1. Why do you think the human race is so intrigued by "the other side of the hedge"? What goes through your mind when people claim to have been to the other side and come back, and when others claim there is nothing beyond the hedge? Why don't the rumors about the other side simply fade away?

2. John Ortberg presents two views of what the essence of the gospel really is: (1) the gospel has to do with the minimal entrance requirements for getting into heaven, or (2) the gospel has to do with Jesus coming to earth and bringing the kingdom of God with him. Discuss the ways each of these views shapes our thinking about God's presence with us and what we can experience in this life *right now*.

3. When Jesus invites us to be his followers, he invites us to experience the goodness of life in the presence of God, but it doesn't end with us. What else does he invite us to do in relationship to other people and the world in which we live?

4. What is the "hedge-breaking business" as John Ortberg describes it? What are some everyday examples of "hedge breaking"?

5. When we are suffering through a season of spiritual winter and find it hard to sense God's presence, how do we know it is okay to complain to God about it?

Group Exploration

John Ortberg writes, "God doesn't reveal himself to us just to make us happy or to deliver us from loneliness. He also comes to us so that we can in turn be conduits of his presence to other people. He invites us to join him in making things down here the way they are up there."

It truly is a privilege not only to live our lives with an awareness of God's presence, but to become conduits of his presence and make "up there" come "down here." It takes conscious effort on our part to live as hedge-breakers, but Scripture gives us plenty of instruction and real-life examples. Let's look at some of those Scripture passages and consider some action points—practical ways in which we can join Jesus in making God's will be done on earth as it is in heaven.

1. Read Romans 15:1–6.

    a. Who is our example for how we should live in relationship with others?

    b. When it comes to our relationships with others, our "neighbors," what is different about the way we interact with people if we are making "up there" come "down here"? What is our purpose for following Jesus?

    c.   Describe some practical ways we can apply the teaching of these verses to our daily interaction with others.

2.   Read Luke 14:12–14.

    a.   Who do we customarily invite to our celebrations?

    b.   If we are bringing "up there" to "down here," who does Jesus tell us to invite, and why?

    c.   In what ways can we honor the poor, the crippled, the lame, and the blind today? How can we bring God's presence into the lives of these and other people who are often overlooked?

3. Read Colossians 3:12–17.

    a. What are the virtues of "up there"? How often do we see these practiced in everyday life?

    b. How would life "down here" be different if we each practiced these virtues as we conducted our daily activities? Give some specific examples.

4. Read 1 Thessalonians 5:15, then Luke 6:27–36.

    a. What does "up there" say to do when we are wronged "down here"? How contrary is that to how we normally live? What kind of an impact would we make if we actually followed these instructions?

    b. What is the reason those who follow Jesus should live this way?

c. Discuss how we can fulfill this teaching in the everyday scenarios we face.

5. Read Ephesians 4:31–32.

a. Which symptoms of "down here" are we to eliminate?

b. With what symptoms of "up there" are we to replace them? Why?

6. What are the characteristics of a life lived in the presence of God? (See Romans 12:9–21.) List them all!

a.   Choose several of these characteristics and talk about how the practice of each of them would make a difference in life "down here."

b.   What does God desire to have happen "down here" (v. 21)? What does this tell you about God?

Personal Journey: To Do Now

1. We live with the awareness that something is on the "other side of the hedge." We can't see it, but we hear whispers and sense that there is something beyond life as we know it.

    a. What are some of the whispers of life beyond the hedge that have been most meaningful to you?

    b. In what way(s) does your awareness of what lies on the other side of the hedge affect your everyday life—your thoughts, your hopes, your interactions with other people? How would you like your daily awareness of and response to the other side of the hedge to be different?

2. Jesus broke through the hedge! He came from the other side to show us that God is closer than we think. Not only does he give us the promise of heaven, but he makes the reality of God's presence and power—the life that exists beyond the hedge—available to us now, in this life!

a. Many Christians view the gospel message as being little more than the minimal entrance requirements for heaven. They miss out on the "living life on earth in the presence of God" portion of the gospel that Jesus says is available *right now.* To what extent have you missed out on the fullness of life with God in the here and now? What needs to change so that you can more fully experience life with God on this side of the hedge?

b. We all go through seasons of spiritual winter when it feels as if God is far away. What encouragement do you find in the fact that God is not offended when we complain to him about how far away he seems to be? What assures you that, even during those times, God is closer than you think?

3. Jesus invites his followers to join him in bringing a little bit of life beyond the hedge to life on earth. It is our privilege to join God in making things "down here" more like the way they are "up there." Every time we pray for heaven to be present on earth, our life becomes the place where God dwells, and that makes all the difference.

a. Ask yourself, "In which areas of my life do I need a beyond-the-hedge infusion? Where do I long to see God's presence and power break into my heart and life?" Write down these needs, and during the coming weeks ask God to reveal his presence to you in these areas.

b. Ask yourself, "Where would I especially like God to use me to make things 'down here' run the way they do 'up there'?" Write down three practical ways in which you can start breaking down the hedge and sharing what's "up there" in heaven with people around you.

God Is Closer Than You Think

John Ortberg

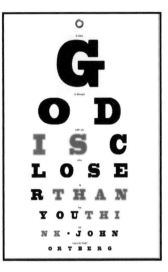

Two works of art help John Ortberg think about the presence of God. One is Michelangelo Buonarroti's brilliant painting of God and Adam on the ceiling of the Sistine Chapel. God is close. His hand comes within a hair's breadth of the hand of the man. It seems to say that God is closer than we think—he's here, now, today, accessible to all who will but "lift a finger."

The second work of art is Martin Hanford's cartoon character Waldo. He is on every page of the Where's Waldo? books, but he can be difficult to find. In the same way, even though God is present on every page of our lives, he's often not easy to spot.

In *God Is Closer Than You Think*, John Ortberg examines this frustrating paradox of the Christian life.

"When it is so easy to 'see' God all around me (in trees, in birds, in nature) why is it so hard to feel his presence—especially when I need him most?"

Ortberg helps readers discover the secret to living daily in the reality of God's most frequent promise in Scripture, "I will be with you."

Hardcover: 0-310-25349-7
ebooks:
Adobe Acrobat eBook Reader® format: 0-310-26336-0
Microsoft Reader® format: 0-310-26337-9
Mobipocket® format: 0-310-26339-5
Palm Reader® format: 0-310-26338-7
Unabridged Audio Pages® CD: 0-310-26379-4
Abridged Audio Pages® CD: 0-310-26450-2

Pick up a copy today at your favorite bookstore!

GRAND RAPIDS, MICHIGAN 49530 USA

WWW.ZONDERVAN.COM

Willow Creek Association

God Is Closer
Than You Think
ZondervanGroupware™
Small Group Edition

John Ortberg with
Stephen & Amanda Sorenson

The story of the Bible is the story of God's
desire to be with his people. God is extending
himself, stretching out to reach us and to fill
our lives with his presence. Every moment of
your life is like a page in a Where's Waldo book. God is there, the Scriptures tell
us, but the ease with which he may be found varies from one page to the next.
God is closer than you think!

The curriculum kit provides sermon resources and promotional materials for
the pastor, small group materials for discussion in groups, and a sample copy of
the hardcover book that everyone can read on their own. The kit includes a six-
session small group participant's guide, a six-session DVD featuring John
Ortberg, a thirty-two-page leader's guide, a CD-ROM with sermon resources
and promotional materials, and one copy of the hardcover book.

Curriculum Kit: 0-310-26635-1
Participant's Guide: 0-310-26639-4
Leader's Guide: 0-310-26640-8

Pick up a copy today at your favorite bookstore!

ZONDERVAN™

GRAND RAPIDS, MICHIGAN 49530 USA
WWW.ZONDERVAN.COM

WILLOW
Willow Creek Association

We want to hear from you. Please send your comments about this book to us in care of zreview@zondervan.com. Thank you.

GRAND RAPIDS, MICHIGAN 49530 USA
WWW.ZONDERVAN.COM